Oscar and George's Adventure

ISBN 979-8-89345-776-6 (paperback)
ISBN 979-8-89345-777-3 (digital)

Christian Faith Publishing
832 Park Avenue
Meadville, PA 16335
www.christianfaithpublishing.com

Printed in the United States of America

Oscar and George's Adventure

Jean Tange

Up on the shelf sat two little bears,
Old and worn and in need of repairs.
One's name was Oscar; he wore a striped tie;
The other was George; he was missing an eye.

Their fur was all tattered, dusty, and old,
But these two bears had true hearts of gold.
They remembered a boy from a long time ago
Who shared adventures with them as he continued to grow.

The bears loved the boy, and the boy loved the bears;
Adventures and games they often would share.
They'd climb trees, skip rocks, and play in the sand,
And at night they'd travel to their favorite dreamland.

But the boy grew up and moved far away.
The bears sat on the shelf and stayed out of the way.
The boy came to visit, but it wasn't the same,
For he was a man now with no time for games.

The boy took a wife and had a child of his own.
The bears were forgotten; they felt all alone.
They were saddened by this, for they missed the boy;
They remembered the good times with thoughts of great joy.

On a day like any other, the door opened wide,
And there stood the man with a child at his side.
The man said to the boy with a smile on his face,
"Son, this is your room now; it's your own special space."

"When I was a boy, I spent lots of time here,
Playing and sleeping and changing each year.
Now with Grandma and Grandpa moving next door,
This house is all yours to love and explore."

The bears' faces lit up when they saw the young boy,
For they knew their lives would be filled with great joy.
They imagined the fun and the times they would have
With this new little boy who looked just like his dad.

The man sat on the bed and looked all around,
On his face was a smile; he made not a sound.
In no time at all, his eyes saw the bears,
And he knew that his son was in the best kind of care.

For he remembered his days with the bears by his side,
And the adventures they'd had near, far, and wide.
They'd climbed trees, caught frogs, and played all kinds of games;
He knew for his son it would be just the same.

When the man and his son turned around and closed the door,
The bears were elated, and they danced on the floor.
They were thrilled that a child was back in their lives
And they laughed, and they hugged, and gave excited high fives.

It wasn't long after that the boy moved to his room,
But instead of being happy, he seemed full of gloom.
He'd lie on his bed and out the window he'd look,
And sometimes he'd cry, and his whole body shook.

The bears hated to see him so sad and upset
That they worried and worried and started to fret.
They had to take action and do it right quick.
They knew what to do; they had just the trick!

When the boy returned home later that day,
The bears jumped off the shelf and said, "Let's play!"
The boy was so startled to hear the bears talk
That all he could do was stare and gawk.

To have two little bears come to life in his room
Was more than the boy could ever assume.
The boy looked at the bears with wide-open eyes,
And in a quiet voice, they heard him say, "Hi."

The boy hugged the bears but then started to sneeze.
"You're dusty and dirty," he started to tease.
The bears knew it was true, for they hadn't been brushed
For ages and ages; they were no longer plush.

The boy grabbed a brush and knew it was time
To brush the bears' fur until it started to shine.
And when he was done, he smoothed Oscar's tie,
And then found a button to fix George's eye.

And after all this, the bears looked brand new,
They turned to the boy and uttered, "Thank you!"
"We've been waiting and waiting for you to appear,
And now we'll be known as the Three Musketeers!"

"A long time ago when your dad was quite small,
We all stood together, all for one and one for all.
So now it's we three; we'll do our very best
To be true to each other and all of the rest."

The boy felt much better; he was no longer sad.
Living in a new place was not all that bad.
He'd left behind his friends and his little old school,
But he felt his new life would turn out way cool.

He slept very soundly and dreamt of the bears.
He woke in the morning without any cares.
But when he opened the door, he heard a loud cry.
He could tell by the sound that it was really nearby.

He yelled, "Oscar and George, you must come right quick,
Someone needs help; this isn't a trick!"
Quick as a flash, George and Oscar appeared,
And the boy told them both what it was that he heard.

They ran to the street to see what was the matter.
In a minute they knew they'd be needing a ladder.
For across the street with a skinned-up knee
Stood a red-headed girl with her kite in a tree.

The boy grabbed the ladder from his parents' backyard,
Then the bears climbed the tree; it wasn't too hard.
They loosened the kite from the leaves of the tree,
And in no time at all, they had set that kite free.

The little girl was so happy—her kite safe and sound,
And she helped the two bears get back on the ground.
But she wasn't quite sure if she believed her own eyes:
Two bears and a boy helping was quite a surprise!

She turned to say, "Thanks," but they were already gone,
So she picked up her kite and walked across the green lawn.
She was glad she yelled, "Help!" and they did appear;
She knew they would help any time of the year.

So that is how the boy and the two bears did meet,
And how they helped the little girl who lived across the street.
More adventures awaited these Three Musketeers;
One never knows when they just might appear.

Until then the bears want to remind all of you
To help each other and do all you can do.
A small act of kindness can make anyone's day,
So don't wait until tomorrow; do a kind act today!

About the Author

After teaching English in rural Montana schools for thirty-three years, Jean retired and decided it was time to write a children's book. She loves to rhyme and knew that the story of two little bears was the perfect place to start. She was introduced to those two bears by her husband, whose father used to tell Oscar and George bedtime stories. She grew up in Montana and currently resides in eastern Montana with her two dogs, Ollie and Blue, and her husband, Carl.

www.ingramcontent.com/pod-product-compliance
Lightning Source LLC
Chambersburg PA
CBHW040203110726
48005CB00018B/2872